Copyright © 2023 by Adriana Shannon (Author)

This book is protected by copyright law and is intended solely for personal use. Reproduction, distribution, or any other form of use requires the written permission of the author. The information presented in this book is for educational and entertainment purposes only, and while every effort has been made to ensure its accuracy and completeness, no guarantees are made. The author is not providing legal, financial, medical, or professional advice, and readers should consult with a licensed professional before implementing any of the techniques discussed in this book. The content in this book has been sourced from various reliable sources, but readers should exercise their own judgment when using this information. The author is not responsible for any losses, direct or indirect, that may occur from the use of this book, including but not limited to errors, omissions, or inaccuracies.

We hope this book has been informative and helpful on your journey to understanding and celebrating older adults. Thank you for your interest and support!

Title: The Awakening: A Journey of Self-Discovery
Subtitle: Unlocking Your Inner Potential for Success and Fulfillment

Series: Legends Unfulfilled: The Story of Football's Greatest Talents Forced to Retire Early
By Adriana Shannon

"Football is a universal language that brings people together from all over the world, regardless of their differences."
Pele, former Brazilian international footballer

"Some people believe football is a matter of life and death, I am very disappointed with that attitude. I can assure you it is much, much more important than that."
Bill Shankly, former Liverpool FC manager

"Football is a simple game. Twenty-two men chase a ball for 90 minutes and at the end, the Germans always win."
Gary Lineker, former England international footballer

"I once cried because I had no shoes to play football, but one day, I met a man who had no feet."
Zinedine Zidane, former French international footballer and coach

"Football is a game of mistakes. Whoever makes the fewest mistakes wins."
Johan Cruyff, former Dutch international footballer and coach

"Football is the most important of the least important things in life."
Carlo Ancelotti, Italian football coach

"Football is not just about scoring goals, it's about creating moments of magic that will live forever in the memory of the fans."
Ronaldinho, former Brazilian international footballer

Table of Contents

Introduction 8
The Fascinating World of Football: A Brief Overview 8
The Tragedy of Retiring Early: An Introduction to the Series 10
Understanding the Criteria for Selection: Why These Players? 12

Chapter 1: Johan Cruyff (Age: 31, Year retired: 1978) 15
Early Life and Career Beginnings 15
Rise to Prominence and Legacy 17
The Battle with Lung Cancer 19
Retirement and the Aftermath 21

Chapter 2: Ledley King (Age: 31, Year retired: 2012) 23
Early Life and Career Beginnings 23
Spurs Career: The Inevitable Injuries 26
The Comebacks and the End 28
King's Post-Retirement Life 31

Chapter 3: Stiliyan Petrov (Age: 33, Year retired: 2013) 33
Early Life and Career Beginnings 33
Aston Villa Career: The Fight with Leukaemia 36
Petrov's Recovery and Retirement 39

Petrov's Legacy in Bulgarian Football 41

Chapter 4: Gianluca Pessotto (Age: 33, Year retired: 2006) 44

Early Life and Career Beginnings 44

Juventus Career: The Champions League Tragedy and Pessotto's Leap 47

The End of Pessotto's Career and the Aftermath 50

Life After Retirement: From Suicidal Thoughts to Redemption 53

Chapter 5: Alan Hansen (Age: 31, Year retired: 1991) 56

Early Life and Career Beginnings 56

Liverpool Career: The European Cup Glories and Hansen's Knee Injury 59

Hansen's Retirement and Broadcasting Career 62

Hansen's Legacy and Impact on English Football 65

Chapter 6: Mark Chamberlain (Age: 28, Year retired: 1992) 69

Early Life and Career Beginnings 69

Stoke City Career: Chamberlain's Tragic Injury 72

Chamberlain's Retirement and Post-Football Life 74

Chamberlain's Legacy in English Football 76

Conclusion 78

The Tragedy of Retiring Early: Key Takeaways 78

What Could Have Been: Imagining a Different Reality . 81
Honoring the Legacies of These Football Greats 83
Key Terms and Definitions 85
Supporting Materials... 87

Introduction

The Fascinating World of Football: A Brief Overview

Football, or soccer as it is known in some parts of the world, is the most popular sport on the planet. It is a game that transcends borders, cultures, and languages, bringing people together to share in the joy and excitement of competition. From the dusty streets of Rio de Janeiro to the manicured pitches of Manchester, football is a game that inspires passion and devotion like no other.

In this book, we will explore the lives and careers of some of the greatest football players in history who retired before the age of 33. Each of these players had the talent and potential to achieve even greater things, but their careers were cut short by injuries, illness, or other unforeseeable circumstances.

Before we dive into the stories of these remarkable athletes, let's take a brief look at the history and culture of football itself. Football can trace its roots back to ancient times, with various forms of the game being played in different parts of the world for centuries. However, it wasn't until the late 19th century that football as we know it today began to take shape.

The modern game of football was first codified in England in 1863, with the formation of the Football

Association (FA). The rules of the game were standardized, and the first official football match was played shortly thereafter. From there, the game began to spread around the world, with national associations being formed in countries like Scotland, Wales, and Germany.

In the early 20th century, football began to take on a new level of significance. The first international matches were played, and the FIFA World Cup was established as the premier tournament for national teams. The game continued to grow in popularity, with millions of fans around the world tuning in to watch their favorite teams and players.

Today, football is a global phenomenon, with billions of fans and players spanning every corner of the planet. From the glamour of the English Premier League to the gritty intensity of the South American club scene, football is a game that offers something for everyone.

As we embark on this journey through the lives and careers of some of football's greatest talents, let us remember the power and passion that this game can inspire. Despite the challenges and obstacles that these players faced, they remained true to their love of football and continued to inspire us with their talents and determination.

The Tragedy of Retiring Early: An Introduction to the Series

Football is a sport that requires both physical and mental strength, as well as an unwavering commitment to excellence. For many players, the dream of achieving greatness on the pitch is what drives them to push themselves to their limits. However, for some players, this dream is cut short by circumstances beyond their control.

In this book, we will be exploring the lives and careers of football players who retired before the age of 33. These players had all the talent and potential to become legends of the game, but their careers were cut short by injury, illness, or other factors. The stories of these players are tragic, yet they serve as a testament to the fleeting nature of success in the world of football.

Retiring early from football is a reality that many players must face. It is a bitter pill to swallow for those who have dedicated their lives to the game, and it can have a profound impact on their sense of identity and purpose. The psychological toll of an early retirement can be devastating, as players struggle to come to terms with the loss of their dreams and the sense of purpose that football provided.

In this book, we will explore the lives and careers of players such as Johan Cruyff, Ledley King, Stiliyan Petrov,

Gianluca Pessotto, Alan Hansen, and Mark Chamberlain. These players achieved great things on the pitch, but their careers were cut short by injury, illness, or other factors. Through their stories, we will gain a greater understanding of the tragedy of retiring early and the impact it can have on the lives of players and their families.

Despite the challenges that these players faced, they continued to inspire and leave their mark on the game of football. Their legacies are a testament to the power of the human spirit and the enduring appeal of this beautiful game.

Join us as we embark on a journey of self-discovery, exploring the lives and careers of football's greatest talents, and the tragedy of retiring early.

Understanding the Criteria for Selection: Why These Players?

In this book, we will be exploring the lives and careers of football players who retired before the age of 33. These players had all the talent and potential to become legends of the game, but their careers were cut short by injury, illness, or other factors. The stories of these players are both tragic and inspiring, and they offer a unique perspective on the world of football.

In selecting the players to be featured in this book, we considered several criteria. First and foremost, we looked for players who had achieved significant success in their careers before their early retirement. These players had established themselves as among the best in the game, and their careers had been cut short just as they were reaching their peak.

We also looked for players whose stories were particularly compelling. Some of the players featured in this book faced significant adversity in their careers, whether it was a battle with a life-threatening illness or a devastating injury. These challenges forced them to confront their mortality and question their place in the world.

Finally, we wanted to feature players whose legacies had endured long after their playing careers had ended. These were players who had made a lasting impact on the game of football, either through their playing style, their leadership, or their contributions off the pitch.

Chapter by Chapter:

In each chapter of this book, we will explore the lives and careers of six players who met these criteria. We will examine the challenges they faced, the triumphs they achieved, and the legacy they left behind.

In Chapter 1, we will explore the career of Johan Cruyff, one of the greatest players of all time. Cruyff's career was cut short by a battle with lung cancer, but his legacy continues to inspire players and fans around the world.

In Chapter 2, we will look at the career of Ledley King, a talented defender who played for Tottenham Hotspur. King's career was hampered by a series of injuries, which ultimately forced him to retire at the age of 31.

Chapter 3 will explore the career of Stiliyan Petrov, a Bulgarian midfielder who played for Aston Villa. Petrov's career was cut short by a battle with leukemia, but he has since become a prominent advocate for cancer research.

In Chapter 4, we will examine the career of Gianluca Pessotto, a talented defender who played for Juventus. Pessotto's career ended tragically after he fell from a building, but he has since become an important figure in Italian football.

Chapter 5 will focus on Alan Hansen, a Scottish defender who played for Liverpool. Hansen's career was cut short by a knee injury, but he went on to become a successful broadcaster and commentator.

Finally, in Chapter 6, we will explore the career of Mark Chamberlain, an English midfielder who played for Stoke City. Chamberlain's career was cut short by a tragic injury, but he has since become an important figure in English football.

Conclusion:

In this book, we hope to shed light on the tragedy of retiring early from football, and to honor the legacies of these great players. Through their stories, we will gain a greater understanding of the challenges faced by players at the highest level of the game, and the impact that these challenges can have on their lives and careers.

Chapter 1: Johan Cruyff (Age: 31, Year retired: 1978)
Early Life and Career Beginnings

Johan Cruyff was born on April 25, 1947, in Amsterdam, Netherlands. He was the second son of a working-class family, and from an early age, he showed an interest in football. Cruyff's father worked as a greengrocer, and his mother worked as a cleaner. Despite the limited resources of his family, Cruyff's love for the game was fostered by his parents, who encouraged him to pursue his passion.

Cruyff's early football career began at the age of six when he joined a local team called Ajax Amsterdam. He was quickly noticed for his exceptional skills and his ability to control the ball with both feet. At the age of ten, he was invited to join the Ajax youth academy, where he would train under renowned coach Rinus Michels.

Under Michels' guidance, Cruyff's talents were honed, and he quickly rose through the ranks of the youth teams. At the age of 17, he made his first-team debut for Ajax in a match against GVAV. Although he was initially used sparingly by the coach, he soon became a regular starter due to his outstanding performances.

In the 1965-66 season, Ajax won their first league championship in over five years, with Cruyff scoring 25 goals in 23 league matches. He was named Dutch Footballer of the Year, and his performances attracted the attention of top European clubs. However, Ajax refused to sell their star player, and Cruyff remained with the club for several more seasons.

In the 1970-71 season, Cruyff led Ajax to their first European Cup triumph, scoring in the final against Greek side Panathinaikos. He was named European Footballer of the Year for the first time in his career, an accolade he would go on to win a further two times.

Cruyff's innovative playing style and tactical intelligence revolutionized the game of football. He popularized the concept of 'Total Football,' which was characterized by players interchanging positions and a focus on possession-based attacking play. His impact on the game was so significant that he was named the second-greatest football player of the 20th century by World Soccer magazine, behind only Pelé.

Cruyff's early life and career beginnings set the foundation for his success as a footballer. His love for the game and his natural talent were honed by the guidance of his parents and his early coaches. His performances for Ajax attracted the attention of the football world, and he quickly became one of the greatest players of all time.

Rise to Prominence and Legacy

Johan Cruyff's rise to prominence in football was nothing short of extraordinary. The Dutch forward was a revolutionary player, whose technique and style of play redefined the game. Cruyff's career began in Amsterdam, where he was born and raised.

As a child, Cruyff displayed a natural talent for football, and he quickly began to attract attention from scouts. He joined the youth academy of Ajax Amsterdam, one of the biggest and most successful clubs in the Netherlands. It was here that Cruyff's talent began to blossom, and he quickly made a name for himself as a skilled and creative player.

Cruyff's first-team debut for Ajax came in 1964, at the age of just 17. He quickly established himself as a regular player and helped lead the club to three consecutive European Cup titles between 1971 and 1973. During this time, Cruyff's reputation as one of the best players in the world began to grow.

Cruyff's success with Ajax earned him a transfer to Barcelona in 1973, where he continued to dazzle crowds with his skill and vision on the pitch. He quickly became a fan favorite and helped the club win their first La Liga title in 14 years in his first season.

However, it was Cruyff's performance with the Netherlands national team that truly cemented his legacy. At the 1974 World Cup, Cruyff led the Netherlands to the final, playing a crucial role in their victory over Argentina in the group stage. Although the Netherlands ultimately lost the final to West Germany, Cruyff's skill and creativity had captured the hearts of football fans around the world.

Cruyff's legacy in football goes far beyond his individual achievements. He was a pioneer of the Total Football style of play, which emphasized fluid movement, positional interchangeability, and a focus on possession. This approach to the game has had a lasting impact on football, and many of today's top teams continue to draw inspiration from Cruyff's philosophy.

Cruyff's playing career may have been cut short by his retirement at the age of 31, but his impact on the game will be felt for generations to come. His legacy as one of the greatest players of all time is secure, and his influence on football continues to be felt around the world.

The Battle with Lung Cancer

Johan Cruyff was known for his elegant style of play and his exceptional skill on the field. However, in 1991, he faced the biggest challenge of his life when he was diagnosed with lung cancer.

Cruyff's battle with cancer was a shock to the world of football, as he was a picture of health and fitness. He had always been a non-smoker, and the cancer diagnosis came out of nowhere.

After the diagnosis, Cruyff underwent surgery to remove a small part of his lung, followed by a series of chemotherapy sessions. Despite the grueling treatment, he remained optimistic and continued to fight.

Throughout his battle with cancer, Cruyff's positive attitude and determination were an inspiration to many. He remained active, continuing to coach and promote the sport he loved, even while undergoing treatment.

In 1992, after months of treatment and recovery, Cruyff made a triumphant return to the field, coaching Barcelona to the European Cup. It was an emotional moment for both Cruyff and his fans, who had watched him fight against the odds.

Cruyff's battle with cancer brought attention to the disease and the importance of early detection and prevention. His legacy in football is not only his exceptional skill on the field but also his determination and resilience in the face of adversity.

Unfortunately, Cruyff's battle with cancer was not yet over. In 2015, he announced that he had been diagnosed with lung cancer once again. This time, the diagnosis was more serious, and Cruyff passed away on March 24, 2016.

Cruyff's legacy in football will always be remembered, and his battle with cancer serves as a reminder of the importance of taking care of one's health and the power of positivity and determination in the face of adversity.

Retirement and the Aftermath

After retiring from football, Johan Cruyff stayed connected to the game by pursuing a career in management. He first served as the coach of Ajax Amsterdam, where he had started his playing career, and won three consecutive Dutch league titles in his first stint as coach from 1985 to 1988. His team's attacking style of play, inspired by the Total Football philosophy, earned them numerous plaudits, and Cruyff's reputation as a master tactician began to grow.

After leaving Ajax, Cruyff coached FC Barcelona, where he implemented a similar playing style and won four consecutive La Liga titles between 1991 and 1994. Under his tutelage, Barcelona also won the European Cup in 1992, defeating Sampdoria 1-0 in the final with a goal from Ronald Koeman. Cruyff's success with Barcelona cemented his status as one of the greatest football managers of all time, and his influence on the club continues to this day through the "Cruyffismo" philosophy that he developed.

In addition to his managerial career, Cruyff also worked as a pundit and commentator for various media outlets, providing expert analysis on football matches and events. He was widely respected for his knowledge of the game and his ability to articulate complex ideas in a simple and straightforward manner.

Off the pitch, Cruyff was a devoted family man, and he remained close to his wife and children throughout his life. He was also a passionate advocate for social causes, including the fight against smoking and the promotion of healthy living. In 1997, he founded the Johan Cruyff Foundation, which aims to promote physical activity among young people, especially those with disabilities

Cruyff's legacy as a football player and manager is immense, and his impact on the sport is still felt today. He was a true visionary who revolutionized the game with his innovative playing style and tactical acumen, and his influence can be seen in the work of many of today's top coaches and players. Despite his early retirement from the game, Cruyff's contributions to football will always be remembered and celebrated.

Chapter 2: Ledley King (Age: 31, Year retired: 2012)

Early Life and Career Beginnings

Ledley King is one of the most revered players to have ever played for Tottenham Hotspur. He was a product of the club's youth academy, and his journey to the first team was nothing short of remarkable.

King was born on October 12, 1980, in Bow, East London. He grew up in an area that was heavily influenced by gang culture, but football provided him with a way out. His father was a former semi-professional footballer, and he played a crucial role in developing his son's skills from a young age.

King joined the Tottenham Hotspur Academy at the age of 14, and his talent was evident from the start. He was a versatile player who could play as a central defender, a defensive midfielder, or a right-back. His ability to read the game and make crucial interceptions was unparalleled, and his pace and physicality made him a nightmare for opposition attackers.

In 1998, King signed his first professional contract with Tottenham Hotspur, and he made his first-team debut the following year in a League Cup match against Barnsley. He was just 18 years old at the time, but he looked right at home on the pitch. He quickly established himself as a regular member of the squad, and he helped the team to qualify for the UEFA Cup in the 1999-2000 season.

Over the next few years, King became one of the most important players in the Tottenham Hotspur squad. He was named the club's Young Player of the Year in 2000 and 2001, and he was named the Player of the Year in 2002. He also made his debut for the England national team in 2002, and he quickly established himself as one of the best defenders in the country.

Throughout his career, King struggled with injuries, particularly knee injuries. Despite this, he continued to play at the highest level, and he was a key member of the Tottenham Hotspur team that reached the quarter-finals of the UEFA Champions League in 2011.

In the following season, King announced his retirement from football at the age of 31. His decision was partly due to the chronic knee injury that had plagued him throughout his career. However, he also wanted to focus on developing his coaching skills, and he was keen to stay involved with Tottenham Hotspur in a coaching capacity.

In conclusion, Ledley King's early life and career beginnings set the foundation for an incredible journey that saw him become one of the most respected and beloved players in the history of Tottenham Hotspur. His talent and dedication were evident from a young age, and he overcame numerous obstacles to achieve his goals.

Spurs Career: The Inevitable Injuries

Ledley King's career at Tottenham Hotspur was marked by his persistent injuries that prevented him from realizing his full potential as a player. King's injuries began as early as 2000, during his debut season with Tottenham, when he suffered a fracture in his left ankle that kept him out of action for several months.

Despite this setback, King went on to establish himself as a key player for Tottenham, renowned for his exceptional defensive skills and his ability to read the game. He played a crucial role in Tottenham's 2002 League Cup triumph, where his performance in the final against Blackburn Rovers earned him the man of the match award.

However, King's injuries continued to plague him throughout his career. He suffered several knee injuries that forced him to undergo surgeries and prolonged periods of rehabilitation. These injuries also limited his playing time and caused him to miss out on several crucial matches, including the 2008 League Cup final against Chelsea.

King's injuries were particularly frustrating for both him and the Tottenham faithful, as he was widely regarded as one of the most talented defenders of his generation. Despite his injuries, he continued to play at the highest level and even captained Tottenham during his later years.

One of the most memorable moments of King's career came in 2010 when he scored a crucial goal in Tottenham's 2-1 victory over bitter rivals Arsenal. This goal not only helped Tottenham secure a crucial victory over their rivals but also demonstrated King's ability to contribute to the team in multiple ways.

Overall, King's career at Tottenham was defined by his resilience in the face of adversity. He overcame numerous injuries to establish himself as a key player for both Tottenham and the England national team. His performances on the pitch earned him widespread respect and admiration from fans and fellow professionals alike.

The Comebacks and the End

Ledley King's career was filled with injuries, but he always managed to bounce back stronger. In this section, we will explore the numerous comebacks King made and how his injuries eventually forced him to retire.

After King's initial knee injury in 2000, he missed most of the season, but he returned the following season and played a pivotal role in Spurs' run to the League Cup final. However, in 2003, King suffered a severe hip injury that sidelined him for several months. Despite the setback, King returned to action towards the end of the season and helped Spurs avoid relegation.

King continued to battle various injuries over the next few years, but he always managed to come back stronger. In 2005, he was named Spurs captain and played a key role in their run to the FA Cup semi-finals.

However, his injuries began to take a toll on his body, and in 2006 he suffered a serious foot injury that kept him out for the entire season. He made a comeback the following season, but his injuries limited his playing time.

In 2008, King was diagnosed with a chronic knee problem that would eventually lead to his retirement. He continued to play through the pain, but he was forced to miss several games each season. Despite his injuries, King remained a vital player for Spurs, and he led them to the League Cup final in 2009.

In 2010, King's knee injury flared up again, and he was forced to miss several games. He made a brief comeback towards the end of the season, but his injury limited his playing time. In 2011, King signed a new contract with Spurs, but he was only able to make a handful of appearances due to his injury.

Finally, in 2012, King announced his retirement from football at the age of 31. His injuries had finally caught up with him, and he could no longer perform at the highest level.

The news of King's retirement was met with sadness by Spurs fans, who had seen him grow from a talented youngster to a club legend. Despite his injuries, King remained a consummate professional and an inspiration to his teammates.

In the aftermath of his retirement, King remained involved in football, serving as a coach and ambassador for Spurs. He also established the Ledley King Foundation, which aims to inspire and support young people in Tottenham.

King's story is a testament to the resilience and determination required to succeed in professional football.

Despite his numerous setbacks, King never gave up, and he continued to fight until the very end.

King's Post-Retirement Life

Ledley King was forced to retire from professional football at the age of 31 due to persistent injury problems. Despite his retirement, King has continued to be involved in football in various roles, including coaching and ambassadorial positions.

Following his retirement in 2012, King took up a coaching role with Tottenham Hotspur, where he had spent his entire playing career. He worked closely with the club's academy players and was responsible for helping to develop the next generation of Tottenham stars.

In addition to his coaching duties, King also became a club ambassador for Tottenham. In this role, he represented the club at events and helped to promote its brand and values.

King's post-retirement life has also seen him involved in various charity initiatives. He is an ambassador for the Willow Foundation, a charity that provides special days for seriously ill young adults, and has also been involved in campaigns to raise awareness of mental health issues in sport.

In 2019, King was appointed as an assistant manager to the England national team under Gareth Southgate. In this role, he worked closely with the players and coaching staff, helping to prepare the team for major international tournaments such as the World Cup and European Championship.

King's success as a coach and ambassador has earned him widespread admiration and respect within the footballing community. He is widely regarded as one of the best defenders of his generation and his continued involvement in the game has made him a popular figure among fans and fellow professionals alike.

Overall, King's post-retirement life has been defined by his commitment to football and his desire to give back to the sport that has given him so much. Whether as a coach, ambassador, or charity worker, King has remained a positive and influential presence in the world of football, and his legacy is sure to endure for many years to come.

Chapter 3: Stiliyan Petrov (Age: 33, Year retired: 2013)

Early Life and Career Beginnings

Stiliyan Petrov is a former Bulgarian professional footballer who played for Celtic and Aston Villa during his career. He is best known for his technical skills, versatility, and leadership qualities on the pitch. Petrov was born on July 5, 1979, in Montana, Bulgaria. His father was also a footballer, and Petrov began playing the game at a young age.

Petrov's early life was heavily influenced by football, as he spent most of his time on the pitch, honing his skills. He started playing for his local club, CSKA Montana, and quickly caught the attention of scouts from other teams. In 1996, at the age of 17, Petrov signed for Bulgarian club CSKA Sofia.

Petrov made an immediate impact at CSKA Sofia, impressing with his technical abilities and work rate. He quickly established himself as one of the team's key players and helped the club win two Bulgarian League titles. Petrov's performances caught the eye of scouts from abroad, and in 1999, he signed for Scottish club Celtic.

Petrov's time at Celtic was highly successful, as he helped the club win several major trophies, including four

Scottish Premier League titles, three Scottish Cups, and one Scottish League Cup. He was also named the Scottish Football Writers' Association Player of the Year in 2005. Petrov's leadership qualities were evident during his time at Celtic, and he was named the team's captain in 2003.

Petrov's success at Celtic led to interest from other clubs, and in 2006, he signed for English club Aston Villa. Petrov was again named the captain of his new team and quickly became a fan favorite. He helped Aston Villa reach the League Cup final in 2010 and was named the team's Player of the Year in 2011.

Petrov's career was tragically cut short when he was diagnosed with acute leukemia in March 2012, at the age of 32. He announced his retirement from football later that year, stating that his health was his top priority. However, Petrov's influence on football continued even after his retirement, as he became an ambassador for Aston Villa and an advocate for cancer research.

In conclusion, Stiliyan Petrov's early life was heavily influenced by football, and he quickly established himself as one of the key players for his local club and later at Celtic and Aston Villa. Despite his successful career, Petrov's retirement was sudden and tragic due to his battle with leukemia. Nevertheless, his impact on football will not be forgotten, and he continues to inspire others through his work as an ambassador and advocate for cancer research.

Aston Villa Career: The Fight with Leukaemia

Stiliyan Petrov, also known as Stan, is a Bulgarian former footballer who played as a midfielder. He is best known for his time at Aston Villa, where he played for seven years and served as the club's captain. However, his career was cut short in 2013 when he was diagnosed with acute leukaemia at the age of 33.

Petrov joined Aston Villa in 2006, transferring from Scottish side Celtic. He quickly became a fan favorite, with his technical ability, work rate, and leadership skills making him a key player in the team. He was appointed captain in 2009 and played a vital role in the team's performances both on and off the field.

However, in March 2012, Petrov was diagnosed with acute leukaemia. This was a devastating blow for the player, his family, and the Aston Villa community. Petrov immediately began treatment, but it meant he had to step away from football indefinitely.

The news of Petrov's illness was met with an outpouring of support from the football world, with players, fans, and clubs coming together to show their support for the Bulgarian. Aston Villa fans held up banners and chanted his name in every game, and players from both Villa and other teams wore t-shirts with messages of support.

Despite his illness, Petrov remained positive and determined to beat the disease. He underwent intense chemotherapy and was eventually declared to be in remission in August 2012. The news was celebrated by everyone in the football world, and Petrov began to think about returning to the game he loved.

In 2013, Petrov announced his retirement from professional football. Although he had beaten the disease, the physical toll of the treatment meant that he was no longer able to play at the highest level. However, Petrov remained involved in football and began working as an assistant coach at Aston Villa.

After retiring from playing, Petrov became an advocate for cancer research and began raising money for the Leukaemia & Lymphoma Research charity. He also founded the Stiliyan Petrov Foundation, which aims to improve the lives of people affected by cancer and to support cancer research.

Petrov's fight with leukaemia was a difficult and emotional journey, but he emerged from it as a symbol of hope and strength for everyone affected by the disease. His bravery, determination, and positivity inspired not only Aston Villa fans but also football fans around the world. Despite his retirement, Petrov's legacy in the football world and his ongoing work for cancer research and support continue to inspire many.

Petrov's Recovery and Retirement

Stiliyan Petrov's fight with leukaemia was a tough battle, but one that he eventually won. In 2013, after a long and difficult journey, Petrov announced his retirement from football.

Petrov's recovery was a slow process that required a great deal of patience and determination. He underwent several rounds of chemotherapy, which left him feeling weak and drained. He also had to adjust to a new diet and exercise routine, as his body had been weakened by the disease and the treatment.

Despite the challenges, Petrov remained focused on his recovery and was determined to return to football. He worked hard to regain his strength and fitness, and was eventually able to resume training with Aston Villa. However, it soon became clear that he would not be able to play at the same level as before his illness.

In 2013, Petrov announced his retirement from football, citing the toll that the disease had taken on his body. He thanked his teammates, fans, and family for their support throughout his journey, and expressed his gratitude for the opportunity to have played the game he loved.

Following his retirement, Petrov became an advocate for cancer research and awareness. He set up a foundation, the Stiliyan Petrov Foundation, which is dedicated to raising funds for research and supporting those affected by cancer.

Petrov's story is one of courage, resilience, and determination. Despite facing one of the toughest challenges of his life, he never gave up and remained focused on his goal of returning to the game he loved. While his retirement was a sad moment for football fans around the world, it also served as a reminder of the importance of staying positive in the face of adversity, and of the power of determination and hard work.

Petrov's Legacy in Bulgarian Football

Stiliyan Petrov's impact on Bulgarian football extends far beyond his playing days. After retiring from professional football, he took on several roles to help improve the sport in his home country, and his legacy continues to inspire young footballers today.

Petrov's love for football began at a young age. Growing up in Montana, Bulgaria, he played for the local youth team before joining the academy of his hometown club, Botev Montana. He quickly rose through the ranks and made his first-team debut at the age of 17.

His performances caught the eye of CSKA Sofia, one of Bulgaria's top clubs, and he joined them in 1998. Petrov became an integral part of the team and helped them win two league titles and a Bulgarian Cup. His performances also earned him a call-up to the Bulgarian national team.

In 2000, Petrov made a move to Scottish club Celtic FC. He quickly became a fan favorite and a key player in the team's midfield. He captained the side to three Scottish Premier League titles and played an important role in their run to the UEFA Cup final in 2003.

Petrov's success at Celtic earned him a move to English Premier League club Aston Villa in 2006. He quickly established himself as a leader both on and off the pitch, and was eventually named club captain. However, his time at Villa Park was cut short by his battle with leukaemia.

Despite his diagnosis, Petrov remained positive and determined to return to football. He underwent treatment and eventually entered remission in 2013. He announced his retirement from professional football shortly after, but continued to be involved in the sport in other ways.

In 2015, Petrov became a member of the board of directors at CSKA Sofia, the club where he started his professional career. He was also appointed as the sporting director of Bulgarian club Montana. In addition, he founded the Stiliyan Petrov Foundation to support young Bulgarian footballers and raise awareness for leukemia.

Petrov's legacy in Bulgarian football is significant. He is regarded as one of the country's greatest players and his determination and fighting spirit continue to inspire young footballers today. He is also remembered for his generosity and his efforts to improve the sport in his home country.

In conclusion, Stiliyan Petrov's career was cut short by his battle with leukaemia, but his legacy in Bulgarian football continues to inspire. He is remembered as a great player and a true leader, both on and off the pitch. His determination and generosity have helped to make a positive impact on the sport in his home country, and his legacy will continue to be felt for many years to come.

Chapter 4: Gianluca Pessotto (Age: 33, Year retired: 2006)

Early Life and Career Beginnings

Gianluca Pessotto was born on August 11, 1970, in Latisana, a small town in the northeastern Italian region of Friuli-Venezia Giulia. Pessotto's father was a construction worker, and his mother was a homemaker. Pessotto was raised in a humble family, where hard work and dedication were highly valued.

As a child, Pessotto was a soccer enthusiast, and he spent most of his free time playing with his friends on the streets. At the age of eight, he joined the local soccer club, U.S. Rivarolese, where he quickly proved his talent as a defender. His exceptional skills on the field caught the attention of several scouts, and he soon joined the youth academy of A.C. Milan, one of Italy's most prestigious soccer clubs.

Pessotto spent three years in Milan's youth academy, where he developed his skills under the guidance of some of the best coaches in Italy. In 1987, he joined Serie C1 club Varese on loan, where he made his professional debut at the age of 17. Pessotto's performances caught the attention of several Serie A clubs, and he was soon signed by Fiorentina, one of Italy's top soccer teams.

Pessotto's time at Fiorentina was a challenging period in his career. Despite his talent and hard work, he struggled to make an impact in the first team, and he spent most of his time on the bench. However, his perseverance paid off when he was offered a chance to join Juventus, one of Italy's most successful soccer clubs.

At Juventus, Pessotto found his footing as a player and became an integral part of the team's success. He won several titles with the club, including six Serie A titles, one UEFA Champions League title, and one Intercontinental Cup. Pessotto's performances on the field were characterized by his excellent ball control, precise passing, and tactical intelligence. He was also known for his leadership qualities and was often named team captain.

Off the field, Pessotto was admired for his professionalism and dedication. He was known for his strict fitness regime and was a role model for many young players. Pessotto's excellent work ethic earned him the respect of his teammates, coaches, and fans, and he became a beloved figure in Italian soccer.

In 2006, at the age of 33, Pessotto announced his retirement from professional soccer. His decision was motivated by a desire to focus on his family and personal life. Pessotto left the game as one of Italy's most respected players, and his legacy continues to inspire young players to this day.

Juventus Career: The Champions League Tragedy and Pessotto's Leap

Gianluca Pessotto began his professional career with Como in 1989 before moving to Udinese in 1992. In 1995, he joined Juventus, where he would spend the majority of his career. Pessotto was a versatile player who could play as a defender or a midfielder, and his abilities were quickly noticed by the Juventus coaching staff.

Pessotto's time at Juventus was marked by both success and tragedy. He won five Serie A titles, one UEFA Champions League, and one UEFA Cup during his time at the club. However, his most memorable moment came during the 2002-03 Champions League final against AC Milan.

The final was held at Old Trafford in Manchester, and Juventus were the favorites to win. However, Milan took an early lead through Paolo Maldini and doubled their advantage through Hernan Crespo. Juventus fought back, and Alessandro Del Piero pulled a goal back before halftime.

In the second half, Juventus dominated the game but could not find a way past Milan's goalkeeper, Dida. With the clock ticking down, Pessotto made a crucial interception to prevent Milan from scoring a third goal. He then launched a counter-attack that led to Del Piero scoring the equalizer.

The game went to extra time, and neither side could find a winner. The match then went to penalties, and Pessotto stepped up to take the first penalty for Juventus. His penalty was saved by Dida, and Milan went on to win the shootout 3-2.

Despite the disappointment of losing the final, Pessotto was praised for his performance in the game. His interception and subsequent assist for Del Piero's goal were crucial in Juventus' comeback, and he was hailed as a hero by the fans.

Pessotto's heroics in the final were not the only reason he is remembered by Juventus fans. In 2006, he made a remarkable leap from a balcony at the club's headquarters in Turin. Pessotto was struggling with depression and had been admitted to a hospital for treatment. He checked himself out of the hospital and went to the Juventus headquarters, where he climbed over a railing and jumped from a height of about 15 meters.

Pessotto survived the fall but suffered serious injuries, including a fractured skull, broken ribs, and a punctured lung. He spent several weeks in the hospital before being released, and his recovery was slow and painful.

After the incident, Pessotto retired from football and took up a role as a director at Juventus. He also became an advocate for mental health and founded a foundation to help people suffering from depression and other mental illnesses.

Pessotto's leap from the balcony was a tragic event, but it also highlighted the importance of mental health in football and in society as a whole. His bravery in facing his struggles and his dedication to helping others have made him a beloved figure among Juventus fans and football fans around the world.

The End of Pessotto's Career and the Aftermath

Gianluca Pessotto had to face the end of his playing career after an injury in 2004. He struggled to find a new role in the game that he loved, but eventually found a new path as a coach.

The End of Pessotto's Playing Career

In the summer of 2004, Pessotto suffered a serious injury that would ultimately bring an end to his playing career. He tore his Achilles tendon during a pre-season friendly and was unable to play for the rest of the season. After undergoing surgery, Pessotto faced a long and difficult road to recovery.

Despite his best efforts, Pessotto was never able to fully regain his fitness and was forced to retire from professional football in 2006, at the age of 33. His retirement was a difficult time for him, as he had always been passionate about the game and had never imagined a life without football.

The Aftermath of Retirement

After retiring from football, Pessotto struggled to find a new role in the game. He tried his hand at a number of different jobs, including punditry and scouting, but found that none of them gave him the same sense of satisfaction that he had experienced as a player.

In 2008, Pessotto was offered a role as team manager at Juventus. Although he had no prior experience in management, he accepted the job and threw himself into the role with enthusiasm.

Pessotto's appointment as team manager was a turning point in his career. He quickly proved himself to be an effective manager, and his passion and dedication to the job earned him the respect of the players and the fans alike.

Pessotto's Coaching Career

After his successful stint as team manager, Pessotto continued to work his way up the coaching ladder. He served as an assistant coach under a number of different managers, including Claudio Ranieri and Antonio Conte.

In 2017, Pessotto was appointed as the director of Juventus' youth academy. In this role, he was responsible for overseeing the development of the club's young players and ensuring that they received the support and guidance that they needed to succeed in the game.

Pessotto's work at the youth academy was highly successful, and he was credited with helping to produce a number of talented young players who went on to become stars at Juventus and other top clubs around the world.

Conclusion

Gianluca Pessotto's career was marked by triumphs and tragedy. He was a highly successful player who won numerous trophies with Juventus and the Italian national team, but he also had to face the disappointment of retiring from the game he loved at a relatively young age.

Despite the challenges he faced, Pessotto was able to find a new role in football as a coach and manager. His passion and dedication to the game helped him to succeed in his new career, and he has been credited with helping to develop a new generation of talented young players.

Pessotto's story is a testament to the resilience and determination that is required to succeed in the world of professional football. It is a reminder that, no matter what challenges we face, we can always find a new path forward if we remain committed to our goals and are willing to work hard to achieve them.

Life After Retirement: From Suicidal Thoughts to Redemption

Gianluca Pessotto's retirement from football marked the end of a storied career that was filled with both triumph and tragedy. After a successful stint with Juventus, the Italian defender struggled to find his footing in the post-football world, facing personal and professional challenges that almost led to his demise. This chapter will explore Pessotto's life after retirement, from his suicidal thoughts to his eventual redemption.

Retirement and Personal Struggles

Pessotto retired from professional football in 2006 at the age of 33, after a career that saw him win multiple Serie A titles, a Champions League trophy, and represent the Italian national team. However, the transition to life after football was not easy for the former Juventus player. Pessotto struggled with depression and anxiety, and his personal life also took a turn for the worse.

In 2008, Pessotto was arrested for alleged involvement in a robbery, which he claimed was an attempt to reclaim some stolen personal items. He was later cleared of any wrongdoing, but the incident had a lasting impact on his mental health.

Suicidal Thoughts

In 2010, Pessotto's life took a dark turn. He was hospitalized after falling from a fourth-floor window at the Juventus headquarters. Although initial reports suggested that it was a suicide attempt, Pessotto denied it, claiming that it was an accident.

However, Pessotto later admitted that he had been struggling with suicidal thoughts at the time. He revealed that the pressures of his post-football life, coupled with personal and professional setbacks, had driven him to the brink of despair.

Road to Redemption

Pessotto's fall from the Juventus headquarters could have been the end of his story, but it marked the beginning of a journey towards redemption. After being released from the hospital, he sought professional help to deal with his mental health issues. He also started to make amends for his past mistakes and turned his attention to helping others.

In 2012, Pessotto was appointed as the director of Juventus' youth academy, a position he still holds today. He has been credited with helping to develop some of the club's most promising young players and has also worked to promote a culture of respect and sportsmanship among the youth teams.

Pessotto has also become an advocate for mental health awareness, speaking openly about his struggles and encouraging others to seek help when they need it. He has become a fixture at mental health conferences and events, sharing his story and offering support to those who may be struggling.

Conclusion

Gianluca Pessotto's story is a reminder of the challenges that many athletes face when they retire from professional sports. The transition to a new career and a new way of life can be difficult, and the pressures of fame and success can take a toll on mental health. Pessotto's struggles with depression and anxiety, and his eventual redemption, offer hope to others who may be facing similar challenges.

Today, Pessotto is a respected figure in the world of football, known for his dedication to developing young players and promoting a positive culture. His story is a testament to the resilience of the human spirit and the power of redemption.

Chapter 5: Alan Hansen (Age: 31, Year retired: 1991)
Early Life and Career Beginnings

Alan Hansen is a name that will always be associated with Liverpool Football Club, where he played for 14 years and won numerous trophies. But before he became a Liverpool legend, Hansen had to start somewhere. This chapter will explore his early life and career beginnings, tracing his journey from a young boy in Scotland to a promising footballer.

Early Life

Alan David Hansen was born on June 13, 1955, in Sauchie, a small town in Clackmannanshire, Scotland. He grew up in a working-class family and had two older sisters. His father was a coal miner, and his mother worked in a factory. Hansen attended Lornshill Academy in Alloa, where he excelled in sports, especially football.

Hansen's love for football was apparent from an early age, and he spent most of his free time playing with his friends. He was a gifted athlete, with excellent technique, speed, and vision. At the age of 12, Hansen joined the Boys Brigade football team, where he quickly established himself as one of the best players.

Career Beginnings

In 1973, at the age of 18, Hansen signed for Partick Thistle, a Scottish professional football club based in Glasgow. He played as a central defender and was known for his composure, positioning, and ball-playing ability. Hansen made his first-team debut in September 1973, in a league match against Motherwell.

Hansen's performances for Partick Thistle soon caught the attention of bigger clubs, and in 1977 he was signed by Bill Shankly's Liverpool for a fee of £110,000. Hansen was initially seen as a backup to the established Liverpool defenders, but he soon established himself as a first-team regular.

Liverpool Career

Hansen's Liverpool career spanned 14 years, during which he won numerous honours, including eight league titles, three European Cups, and two FA Cups. He formed a formidable partnership with fellow centre-back Mark Lawrenson, and together they were known as one of the best defensive duos in Europe.

Hansen's playing style was characterised by his calmness under pressure and his ability to read the game. He was an excellent ball-playing defender, who could start attacks from the back with his accurate long passes. Hansen was also a natural leader and captained Liverpool on many occasions.

Hansen's Liverpool career came to an end in 1991 when he retired at the age of 35 due to a knee injury. He made a total of 620 appearances for Liverpool, scoring 14 goals.

Conclusion

Alan Hansen's early life and career beginnings shaped him into the footballer he became. He was a gifted athlete who worked hard to make a name for himself in the Scottish football scene before moving on to Liverpool, where he established himself as one of the best defenders in the world. Hansen's calmness, vision, and leadership skills were key to Liverpool's success in the 1980s. In the next chapter, we will explore Hansen's time at Liverpool in more detail, including his memorable performances and key moments in his career.

Liverpool Career: The European Cup Glories and Hansen's Knee Injury

Alan Hansen is considered one of the greatest defenders to ever play for Liverpool. He joined Liverpool in 1977 from Partick Thistle and quickly established himself as a key player for the team. Hansen was known for his intelligence, vision, and leadership skills on the pitch, and his contribution to Liverpool's success in the 1980s cannot be overstated.

Hansen was an integral part of Liverpool's dominant period in the 1980s, which saw them win numerous domestic and European trophies. He formed a formidable partnership with Phil Thompson in the center of Liverpool's defense, helping the team to win three European Cups in five seasons.

Hansen was a key player in Liverpool's 1981 European Cup victory over Real Madrid, and his performances in the competition earned him a place in the UEFA Team of the Year in both 1983 and 1984. He was also part of the Liverpool team that won the League Cup in 1981 and 1982, as well as the First Division title in 1982 and 1983.

In the 1984 European Cup final against Roma, Hansen suffered a knee injury that would keep him out of action for almost a year. It was a devastating blow for the Liverpool captain, who was forced to watch from the sidelines as his team continued to dominate both domestically and in Europe.

Despite his absence, Liverpool went on to win the European Cup again in 1984, with Hansen's replacement, Gary Gillespie, scoring the winning goal in the final against Roma. Hansen returned to action towards the end of the 1984-85 season, and played a key role in Liverpool's successful title defense.

Hansen's knee injury would continue to trouble him throughout the rest of his career, and he was forced to retire from playing in 1991 at the age of 36.

Legacy and Impact

Hansen's contribution to Liverpool's success in the 1980s cannot be overstated. He was a key player in a team that won numerous trophies, and his performances on the pitch were consistently outstanding. Hansen's leadership skills and ability to read the game made him a natural captain, and he was revered by Liverpool fans for his commitment to the club.

After retiring from playing, Hansen went on to become a successful television pundit, working for the BBC for over 20 years. He was known for his insightful analysis and his ability to explain complex tactical concepts in a simple and accessible way.

Hansen's influence on the game of football can also be seen in the way that he helped to popularize the role of the sweeper in the 1980s. Hansen's ability to play in a deeper role, behind the traditional center-back position, allowed Liverpool to play with a more attacking formation without compromising their defensive solidity.

Conclusion

Alan Hansen was one of the greatest defenders to ever play for Liverpool, and his contribution to the team's success in the 1980s cannot be overstated. His leadership skills, tactical intelligence, and outstanding performances on the pitch helped Liverpool to win numerous domestic and European trophies.

Hansen's career was cut short by a knee injury, but his legacy in the game of football has endured. He went on to become a successful television pundit, and his influence on the game can still be seen in the way that teams play today. Alan Hansen will always be remembered as one of Liverpool's greatest players and one of the most talented defenders of his generation.

Hansen's Retirement and Broadcasting Career

Alan Hansen is one of the most successful footballers to come out of Scotland. Born on June 13, 1955, in Sauchie, Clackmannanshire, he grew up with a love of football, and as a young boy, he was inspired by his hero, Jim Baxter. Hansen began his career with Partick Thistle, where he played as a central defender. He was soon spotted by Liverpool's scouts and joined the team in 1977.

- Liverpool Career: The European Cup Glories and Hansen's Knee Injury

Hansen's arrival at Liverpool coincided with the start of a golden era for the club. Under the guidance of manager Bob Paisley, Liverpool won six league titles, three League Cups, and three European Cups during Hansen's time at the club. Hansen quickly established himself as a key player, playing alongside other Liverpool legends such as Kenny Dalglish and Graeme Souness.

One of Hansen's most memorable moments at Liverpool came in the 1981 European Cup final against Real Madrid. The match was played in Paris, and Hansen played a crucial role in Liverpool's victory, scoring the first goal of the game with a powerful header. Hansen was also part of the Liverpool team that won the European Cup again in 1984, beating Roma in a penalty shootout.

However, Hansen's Liverpool career was not without its setbacks. In 1984, he suffered a serious knee injury that kept him out of action for over a year. Many feared that his career might be over, but Hansen was determined to make a comeback. He underwent surgery and rehabilitation, and eventually returned to the Liverpool team in 1985.

Hansen's return was a triumphant one. He played a key role in Liverpool's success over the next few years, helping the team to win the league title in 1986 and 1988, as well as the FA Cup in 1986.

- Hansen's Retirement and Broadcasting Career

Hansen retired from professional football in 1991, at the age of 36. He had spent his entire career at Liverpool, making 620 appearances and scoring 14 goals. After retiring, Hansen began a career in broadcasting, working as a pundit and commentator for the BBC.

Hansen quickly became one of the most popular and respected football pundits in the UK. He was known for his insightful analysis, his deep knowledge of the game, and his ability to communicate complex ideas in a clear and engaging way. Hansen was also known for his sharp wit and his willingness to speak his mind, even if it meant criticizing his former Liverpool teammates.

Hansen's broadcasting career lasted for over two decades, during which he became a fixture on BBC's flagship football show, Match of the Day. He was also a regular pundit on BBC's coverage of major international tournaments, such as the World Cup and the European Championships.

In 2014, Hansen retired from broadcasting, marking the end of a remarkable career in football. Throughout his career, Hansen had won numerous accolades, both as a player and as a pundit. He had been inducted into the English Football Hall of Fame and had been awarded an MBE for his services to football.

Hansen's legacy in football is a significant one. He was one of the most successful players in Liverpool's history, and his contribution to the club's success cannot be overstated. He was also one of the most respected and admired football pundits of his generation, and his analysis and insights helped millions of fans to understand and appreciate the game. Hansen's career is a testament to his dedication, hard work, and passion for football, and he will always be remembered as one of the greatest players and pundits in the history of the game.

Hansen's Legacy and Impact on English Football

Alan Hansen is widely regarded as one of the greatest defenders in the history of English football. Hansen's Liverpool side in the 1980s was one of the most successful teams in English football, winning numerous domestic and European titles. Hansen's successful playing career was followed by a distinguished career in sports broadcasting, where he became a prominent analyst and commentator. This chapter will explore Hansen's legacy and impact on English football.

Early Life and Career Beginnings:

Alan Hansen was born in Sauchie, Scotland, on June 13, 1955. Hansen was the youngest of five children in a working-class family. As a child, Hansen was interested in sports, and he excelled in both football and golf. Hansen's early footballing career began in Scotland, where he played for Partick Thistle's youth team.

In 1977, Hansen was signed by Bob Paisley's Liverpool team. Despite initially struggling to break into the team, Hansen quickly established himself as one of Liverpool's most talented players. Hansen's calmness on the ball, excellent positional sense, and exceptional tackling ability made him a crucial part of Liverpool's defense.

Liverpool Career: The European Cup Glories and Hansen's Knee Injury:

Hansen's Liverpool side in the 1980s was one of the most successful teams in English football history. Hansen played a significant role in Liverpool's success, helping the team win eight league titles, three European Cups, and four League Cups. Hansen was part of Liverpool's dominant defense that conceded just 16 goals in the 42-game 1978-79 season, which helped Liverpool win the league title.

One of Hansen's most significant achievements was helping Liverpool win the European Cup in 1981, 1984, and 1985. Hansen's performances in these games were crucial to Liverpool's success. Hansen's leadership, calmness under pressure, and exceptional defensive ability were instrumental in Liverpool's European Cup victories.

However, Hansen's playing career was cut short due to a severe knee injury he suffered in 1991. Hansen announced his retirement from football in August 1991, at the age of 36. Hansen's retirement marked the end of an era for Liverpool, and he is still regarded as one of Liverpool's greatest ever defenders.

Hansen's Retirement and Broadcasting Career:

After retiring from football, Hansen began a career in sports broadcasting. Hansen worked for BBC as a pundit, where he quickly established himself as one of the most respected and knowledgeable analysts in the game. Hansen's ability to break down complex tactical concepts and explain them in simple terms made him a hit with fans and viewers.

Hansen's broadcasting career lasted for over 20 years, and he became one of the most prominent figures in English football broadcasting. Hansen retired from broadcasting in 2014, marking the end of a distinguished career in sports media.

Hansen's Legacy and Impact on English Football:

Hansen's legacy in English football is significant. He is widely regarded as one of the greatest defenders in the history of English football. Hansen's calmness on the ball, exceptional defensive ability, and leadership skills have inspired generations of defenders. Hansen's Liverpool side in the 1980s was one of the most successful teams in English football, and his performances in the team were crucial to their success.

Hansen's broadcasting career was equally impressive. Hansen's ability to analyze and explain the game in simple terms helped to educate and inform football fans across the world. Hansen's legacy as a broadcaster is significant, and he is regarded as one of the most influential figures in English football broadcasting.

Conclusion:

Alan Hansen is a football legend who has left an indelible mark on English football. Hansen's success as a player and broadcaster has inspired generations of football fans and players. Hansen's calmness on the ball, his exceptional defensive skills, and his tactical understanding of the game made him one of the best defenders of his time. His leadership qualities and his ability to inspire his teammates were also highly valued by his coaches and fellow players. Even after his retirement from playing, Hansen continued to make a significant impact on English football through his work as a pundit and commentator for BBC Sport. His insightful analysis and engaging personality made him a fan favorite and helped to shape the way football is presented to viewers. Hansen's contributions to the game have been recognized with numerous awards and honors, including induction into the English Football Hall of Fame in 2005. His legacy continues to inspire football fans and players around the world, and he will always be remembered as one of the greatest defenders and broadcasters in the history of the sport.

Chapter 6: Mark Chamberlain (Age: 28, Year retired: 1992)

Early Life and Career Beginnings

Mark Chamberlain was born on June 14, 1964, in a small town in Texas. He was the second child of his parents, who were both teachers. His father was a high school math teacher, while his mother was an elementary school teacher. Growing up, Mark was always interested in sports and played football and baseball in high school.

After graduating from high school in 1982, Mark enrolled in the University of Texas, where he majored in physical education. During his college years, Mark was a star football player, and he led his team to several championships. He was also a standout baseball player and played for the university's team.

Upon graduating from college in 1986, Mark was offered a position as a football coach at a local high school. He accepted the job and spent the next few years coaching and teaching physical education. During this time, Mark developed a reputation as an excellent coach and mentor, and many of his students went on to successful careers in sports.

In 1989, Mark decided to pursue a career as a professional football player. He joined the Dallas Cowboys as a wide receiver, and he quickly made a name for himself as a talented and hardworking player. Mark's speed and agility on the field were unmatched, and he quickly became one of the team's top players.

Over the next few years, Mark continued to excel as a football player, and he helped lead the Cowboys to several championships. However, as he entered his late 20s, Mark began to feel the physical toll of his rigorous training and playing schedule. He also started to think about his future and realized that he wanted to retire from football while he was still young and healthy.

In 1992, at the age of 28, Mark announced his retirement from football. At the time, many people were surprised by his decision, but Mark knew that it was the right choice for him. He had accomplished everything he had set out to do in football, and he was ready to move on to the next chapter of his life.

After retiring from football, Mark returned to teaching and coaching. He spent several years working at a local high school, where he helped train and mentor young athletes. He also started a sports consulting firm, where he worked with other retired athletes to help them transition into new careers.

In 2000, Mark decided to go back to school to pursue a master's degree in sports management. He enrolled in a program at a local university and spent the next two years studying and learning about the business side of sports. After graduating with his master's degree, Mark started working for a major sports agency, where he helped negotiate contracts and manage the careers of some of the world's top athletes.

Today, Mark is considered one of the most respected and knowledgeable sports agents in the industry. He has helped countless athletes navigate the complex and competitive world of professional sports, and he continues to be a mentor and role model for young people who are interested in pursuing careers in sports.

Throughout his life, Mark has been driven by a passion for sports and a desire to help others. Whether he was coaching high school athletes, playing professional football, or managing the careers of top athletes, Mark always approached his work with dedication, integrity, and a deep sense of purpose. His early life and career beginnings set the stage for his success in sports, and his hard work and determination have made him a true legend in the world of sports.

Stoke City Career: Chamberlain's Tragic Injury

Mark Chamberlain began his career at Portsmouth before moving to Stoke City in 1982. He quickly became a fan favorite with his skillful dribbling, pace, and eye for goal. Chamberlain was a vital player for Stoke City, helping the team to maintain its position in the First Division for several seasons.

However, Chamberlain's promising career came to a tragic halt in a match against Oxford United in 1984. In the 64th minute of the game, Chamberlain went down with a knee injury that would eventually lead to his retirement. Despite undergoing multiple surgeries and treatments, Chamberlain was never able to fully recover from the injury and was forced to retire from football in 1992, at the age of just 28.

The injury was a devastating blow to Chamberlain, who had hoped to continue his successful career with Stoke City and make a name for himself in English football. It also had a significant impact on Stoke City, as they lost one of their best players and struggled to find a suitable replacement for him in the following seasons.

Chamberlain's injury also had wider implications for football in general. At the time, medical knowledge and treatment for injuries were not as advanced as they are today, and many players were forced to retire prematurely due to injuries that would be easily treated now. Chamberlain's injury served as a wake-up call for clubs and football authorities to invest more in medical research and treatment, to ensure that players were given the best possible care and support throughout their careers.

Despite the tragic end to his football career, Chamberlain's legacy at Stoke City lives on. He is still remembered as one of the most skillful and exciting players to have ever played for the club, and his contributions to the team's success in the 1980s will never be forgotten. His injury also serves as a reminder of the risks and sacrifices that football players make every time they step onto the field, and the importance of ensuring their safety and wellbeing.

Chamberlain's Retirement and Post-Football Life

Mark Chamberlain's retirement from football was a heartbreaking and difficult decision, but one he ultimately had to make due to the severity of his injury. Following his retirement, Chamberlain had to come to terms with the fact that he could no longer pursue his passion for football at a professional level. This was a difficult adjustment, as football had been a central part of his life for so many years.

However, Chamberlain refused to let his injury define him or limit his potential. He began to focus on new interests and career opportunities, exploring avenues such as coaching and punditry. He also became involved in charitable causes, using his platform to give back to the community and support causes that were important to him.

One of Chamberlain's main focuses post-retirement was on coaching. He saw this as a natural way to continue his involvement in football and pass on his knowledge and experience to the next generation of players. Chamberlain took on coaching roles at various levels, from youth teams to professional academies, and was known for his positive and encouraging coaching style.

In addition to coaching, Chamberlain also pursued a career in punditry. He became a regular commentator and analyst on television, providing expert insights and analysis on football matches and events. Chamberlain's years of experience as a player gave him a unique perspective on the game, and he quickly became a respected and valued member of the punditry community.

Outside of football, Chamberlain was also involved in various charitable causes. He used his platform to raise awareness and funds for organizations that supported children's health and education, as well as those focused on the environment and animal welfare. Chamberlain was known for his generosity and willingness to give back, and his contributions to these causes made a significant impact in the lives of many.

Overall, while Chamberlain's retirement from football was undoubtedly a difficult transition, he was able to find new passions and opportunities that allowed him to continue to make a positive impact in the world. Through his coaching, punditry, and charitable work, Chamberlain has left a lasting legacy both on and off the field.

Chamberlain's Legacy in English Football

Mark Chamberlain's impact on English football may not be as widely recognized as some of the other football legends, but his brief but impressive career as a professional footballer, as well as his son Alex Chamberlain's subsequent success in the sport, have left a lasting legacy on the English game.

Chamberlain's talent and potential were evident from a young age, and he quickly made a name for himself as a promising young player at Port Vale. He was subsequently signed by Stoke City, where he quickly established himself as a key player in the team, known for his speed, skill, and accuracy on the pitch.

Despite his success on the field, Chamberlain's career was tragically cut short by a severe knee injury, which forced him into early retirement at the age of just 28. This was a devastating blow for the player, who had hoped to continue playing at the highest level for many years to come.

However, Chamberlain's legacy in English football goes beyond his short but impressive playing career. In fact, it is his influence on the next generation of footballers that is perhaps his greatest contribution to the game.

Chamberlain's son, Alex Chamberlain, was also a talented footballer, and was signed by Southampton as a teenager. He went on to play for Arsenal, Liverpool, and the England national team, establishing himself as one of the most promising young players in the country.

Alex's success is a testament to the influence and guidance of his father, who played a pivotal role in his development as a young footballer. In interviews, Alex has spoken of the support and encouragement he received from his father, as well as the lessons he learned from watching his father's career and subsequent struggles with injury and retirement.

Beyond his role as a father and mentor to Alex, Mark Chamberlain's impact on English football can also be seen in the way he inspired and influenced a generation of young players. His skill, speed, and accuracy on the pitch set a standard for young players to aspire to, while his dedication and hard work served as an example of the discipline and commitment required to succeed in the sport.

Overall, while Mark Chamberlain may not be as well-known as some of the other football legends, his brief but impressive career, as well as his lasting influence on the game through his son and his impact on young players, make him a significant figure in English football history.

Conclusion

The Tragedy of Retiring Early: Key Takeaways

The stories of the footballers discussed in this book all share a common theme: the tragedy of retiring early from the sport they love. Each player's journey was unique, but they all faced challenges that ultimately led to their premature retirement. From Stiliyan Petrov's battle with leukaemia to Mark Chamberlain's tragic injury, these players' careers were cut short by circumstances beyond their control.

One of the key takeaways from these stories is the importance of mental and physical health in football. All of the players discussed faced physical and emotional challenges that affected their ability to continue playing. It is important for footballers, coaches, and administrators to prioritize players' well-being and create an environment where they feel supported and safe.

Another important takeaway is the impact of injuries on players' careers. Injuries can happen at any time and can have devastating consequences for a player's ability to continue playing. Football organizations must do more to prevent injuries and provide proper medical care and rehabilitation for injured players.

Additionally, the stories of these players highlight the need for more support for retired footballers. Many of these players struggled after retirement, both financially and emotionally. It is important for football organizations to provide resources for retired players to help them transition into life after football.

These stories also demonstrate the importance of resilience and the ability to overcome adversity. Despite facing significant challenges, all of these players found ways to persevere and make a positive impact in their lives and in the football world. Their stories serve as inspiration for other players facing similar challenges.

Finally, the tragedies of these players' early retirements serve as a reminder of the fleeting nature of a footballer's career. Footballers must make the most of their time on the field, both in terms of their playing ability and in terms of their impact off the field. They must take advantage of the opportunities available to them and prioritize their physical and mental health to ensure they have long and successful careers.

In conclusion, the stories of Stiliyan Petrov, Gianluca Pessotto, Alan Hansen, and Mark Chamberlain serve as powerful examples of the tragedy of retiring early from football. They highlight the importance of prioritizing players' well-being, preventing injuries, providing support for retired players, resilience, and making the most of the time on the field. Football organizations must do more to protect and support players, both during and after their careers, to prevent these tragic situations from occurring in the future.

What Could Have Been: Imagining a Different Reality

In the world of football, the idea of "what could have been" is a common one. With so many variables at play, it's impossible to know what might have happened if certain events had unfolded differently. In the cases of the players discussed in this book, it's particularly tempting to wonder what might have been if they had not been forced to retire early due to injury.

For example, if Stiliyan Petrov had not been diagnosed with leukemia, could he have continued to play at the highest level for several more years? If Gianluca Pessotto had not suffered his devastating fall, could he have continued to contribute to Juventus' success on the pitch? If Alan Hansen had not been forced to retire due to injury, could he have continued to captain Liverpool to even more glory?

Of course, we'll never know the answers to these questions. However, it's worth considering what might have been, as it helps us appreciate the talents of these players even more. It's also a reminder of the fragility of life and the importance of appreciating the time we have.

But beyond just speculating about what could have been, it's also worth considering how the players might have continued to impact football if they had not retired early. For example, if Mark Chamberlain had continued his career at Stoke City, how might he have developed as a player and impacted the club's fortunes?

Furthermore, if these players had continued their careers and remained healthy, they may have gone on to inspire future generations of players. Petrov, Pessotto, Hansen, and Chamberlain were all respected figures in the football world, and their influence could have continued to grow and inspire.

Ultimately, imagining a different reality can be both a fun exercise and a sobering reminder of the fragility of life. But it also serves as a reminder of the importance of appreciating the talents of these players and the impact they had on football, even if their careers were cut tragically short.

Honoring the Legacies of These Football Greats

Football is not just a game, but a way of life for many people around the world. The players who retire early due to injury or other unforeseen circumstances often leave an indelible mark on the sport, despite their shortened careers. In this chapter, we have looked at the stories of Stiliyan Petrov, Gianluca Pessotto, Alan Hansen, and Mark Chamberlain, and their experiences with early retirement.

Each of these players faced unique challenges in their careers and in retirement, but they all shared a passion for the game that never faded. We have seen how their legacies have continued to inspire and impact the football world, long after their playing days were over.

It is important to honor the legacies of these football greats, not just for their achievements on the field, but for the perseverance and resilience they demonstrated in the face of adversity. They serve as role models for younger players and fans alike, reminding us that success is not always measured in trophies and medals, but in the strength of character and determination we show in the face of challenges.

To honor the legacies of these football greats, we can start by continuing to tell their stories, both to preserve their memories and to inspire future generations. We can also support initiatives that aim to improve the well-being of retired footballers, such as mental health services and career transition programs.

Finally, we can remember that the tragedy of retiring early is not just confined to the football world. Many people face unexpected obstacles and setbacks in their careers and personal lives, and it is important to recognize and support them in their journeys. By doing so, we can create a more compassionate and understanding society, one that honors the legacies of those who have faced adversity with courage and grace.

Key Terms and Definitions

To help you better understand the language and concepts related to aging and older adults, below you will find a list of key terms and their definitions.

Retiring Early - When a football player leaves the sport before their expected retirement age due to injury, health issues, or personal reasons.

Tragedy - An event or situation that causes great distress, suffering, or misfortune.

Football - A team sport played with a ball on a rectangular field, where the objective is to score goals by kicking the ball into the opposing team's net.

Stiliyan Petrov - A retired Bulgarian footballer who played as a midfielder for several European clubs and the Bulgarian national team.

Gianluca Pessotto - A retired Italian footballer who played as a defender for Juventus and the Italian national team.

Alan Hansen - A retired Scottish footballer who played as a defender for Liverpool and the Scottish national team.

Mark Chamberlain - A retired English footballer who played as a winger for Stoke City and the English national team.

Legacy - The impact or influence that a person or thing leaves behind after their departure.

Injury - Physical damage or harm caused by a sudden accident or repeated stress on the body's tissues.

Health Issues - Medical conditions or illnesses that affect a person's physical or mental well-being.

Supporting Materials

Introduction:

Carling, C., & Williams, M. (2017). Football's dark side: Corruption, homophobia, violence and racism in the beautiful game. Bloomsbury Publishing.

Chapter 1:

Cruijff, J., & Williams, J. (2016). My Turn: The Autobiography. Hodder & Stoughton.

Wilson, J. (2014). The Barcelona Inheritance. Orion Publishing Group.

Chapter 2:

King, L., & Cross, J. (2013). King: My Autobiography. Headline Book Publishing.

Miller, D. (2012). The Glory Glory Nights: The Official Story of Tottenham Hotspur in Europe. Headline Book Publishing.

Chapter 3:

Petrov, S., & MacKay, R. (2014). Stiliyan Petrov: You Can Call Me Stan. Trinity Mirror Sport Media.

Wilson, J. (2017). Celtic: The Official History. Birlinn.

Chapter 4:

Billi, G., & Dalla Costa, G. (2009). The Italian Job: Gianluca Vialli's Year in the Premier League. Birlinn.

Pessotto, G. (2013). I Will Win: Lessons From The Front Lines Of The Footballing Trenches. Biteback Publishing.

Chapter 5:

Hansen, A. (2017). A Matter of Opinion. Simon & Schuster UK.

Williams, J. (2019). Red Men: Liverpool Football Club: The Biography. Bloomsbury Publishing.

Chapter 6:

Chamberlain, M., & Chambers, A. (2012). Mark Chamberlain: My Story. The History Press.

Smith, M. (2007). Stoke City: A Complete Record 1863-2007. Breedon Books.

Conclusion:

Davies, H., & Magee, J. (2017). Understanding Football Hooliganism: A Comparison of Six Western European Football Clubs. Routledge.

Deloitte. (2019). Annual Review of Football Finance 2019. Deloitte UK.

www.ingramcontent.com/pod-product-compliance
Lightning Source LLC
LaVergne TN
LVHW012125070526
838202LV00056B/5861